BARCELONA
THEN & NOW

BARCELONA
THEN & NOW

JOSÉ SOLER

THUNDER BAY
P·R·E·S·S

San Diego, California

Thunder Bay Press
An imprint of the Advantage Publishers Group
5880 Oberlin Drive, San Diego, CA 92121-4794
www.thunderbaybooks.com

Produced by PRC Publishing,
an imprint of Anova Books Ltd,
151 Freston Road,
London W10 6TH, United Kingdom

ISBN-13: 978-1-59223-657-2
ISBN-10: 1-59223-657-X

Library of Congress Cataloging-in-Publication Data available on request

Printed and bound in China

1 2 3 4 5 10 09 08 07 06

ACKNOWLEDGMENTS

I would like to thank the various photo archives that have assisted me in my picture research for this book.
Many thanks to Eulàlia at Arxiu Mas and Mireia at Institut d'Estudis Fotogràfics de Catalunya. I could not
have written this book without the help of my wife, Melissa Cokely, who helped me through the entire
process. Her spirit, as well as my own, can be found in the pages of this work.

José Soler founded Pepito Tours to share his love of Barcelona with people from all over the world. Pepito
Tours specializes in chauffeured and walking tours of Barcelona and the surrounding areas. You can contact
José through his web site www.pepitotours.com.

PICTURE CREDITS

The publisher wishes to thank the following for kindly supplying the photographs that appear in this book:

Then photographs:
Arxiu Històric de la Ciutat de Barcelona – Arxiu Fotogràfic:
Castellà, Enric: 6; Estorch, Joan: 8; Desconegut: 10, 20, 28, 36, 40, 44, 64, 68, 92, 96, 100, 102, 104, 120,
128, 136, 138; Branguli, Josep: 22, 24, 38, 114, 126; Martí, Joan: 30; Ritma: 34; Toldrà Viazo, Angel: 42; J.
E. Puig: 46; Sala: 48; Ballell, Frederic: 50, 66, 72, 74, 84, 110; Esplugas, Antoni: 52, 54, 58; Comas,
Agustín: 60; Dominguez, Josep: 62, 82, 98, 106, 134; Unknown: 76; Toldrà Viazo, Angel: 78; Pérez de
Rozas: 80; Puig, Esteve: 112; Zerkowitz, Adolfo: 116; Pérez de Rozas: 118, 122; Girau Iglesias, Luis: 124.
Institute Amatller d'Art Hispanic. Arxiu Mas: 14 [cb2670], 16 [cb4022], 86 [g-69728], 88 [00366013
re666], 90 [c4977], 94 [00876004 negatiu b-1043].
Arxiu Historic Fotogràfic de L'instut d'Estudis Fotogràfics de Catalunya: 12 [acm-9-4827], 18 [acm-9-
4368p], 26 [acm-9-3881v], 32 [acm-9-4874v], 56 [acm-9-4508p], 70 [acm-9-4010], 108 [acm-9-5283baixa],
130 [acm-9-3030v], 132 [acm-9-34870v], 140[acm-32990v], 142 [acm-14-111].

Now photographs:
All Now images were taken by David Watts (© Anova Image Library) except for the following:
© Massimo Ripani/4Corners Images: 143.

INTRODUCTION

Proud Barcelona residents often say, "We have the sea and the mountains. What more could you want?" The city on the Mediterranean sea, backed by Mount Tibidabo, certainly has the best of both worlds. It is often said that Catalan people can be characterized by two things, *seny* and *rauxa*. Loosely translated this means that Catalans possess both a sense of innate and steadfast order coupled with a spirit of vivacity and a passionate appreciation of life and art. These two apparently contradictory traits have meshed in the city of Barcelona, and this duality marks the daily pulse of the city. Nowhere as in Barcelona can you find the irresistible combination of *seny* ("common sense") and *rauxa* ("ebullient gaiety") that so well defines the Catalan people. This delightful contrast manifests itself in every aspect of the city, from the citizens both now and throughout Barcelona's history, to the architecture and urban planning, as well as the geography.

The region of Catalunya, whose capital is Barcelona, is known among fellow Spaniards as one of the most "serious" cities in the country. Catalans have a reputation for being hardworking and business savvy, and Catalunya is a very prosperous region of Spain. Barcelona is a hotspot not only for tourists but for international commerce as well. Early every morning from Monday to Friday the city is crowded with elegantly dressed business people on their way to work. By night, however, the same hardworking Barcelonans transform into laid-back revellers who enjoy the festivals, outdoor activities, and innumerable bars and restaurants that fill the streets and squares of Barcelona.

The history of the city is also a study in contrasts. Barcelona's historic center, Ciutat Vella, or " the old city," was a maze of narrow streets surrounded by thick walls to protect it from invaders. The lines of the ancient city, as well as pieces of its original walls, are preserved in the narrow winding streets of the Gothic Quarter. Not until 1850 did the conception of Barcelona as we know it begin to take shape. The Expansion, or Eixample, was the result of a massive and meticulously planned project to extend Barcelona beyond the medieval walls and would end up connecting the city with towns such as Horta, Gracia, Sant Andreu, Sarriá, and Sants, absorbing them into the city and transforming them into districts.

With the dawn of the industrial era and its ensuing textile factories, Barcelona's upper class required new, larger living spaces far from the crowded old district, and were given the orderly and elegant apartment buildings of the Eixample project. The Eixample neighborhood is a textbook manifestation of the contrasts of Barcelona, with its carefully gridded streets housing some of the most brilliant and chaotic architectural

masterpieces in the world. The Eixample coincided neatly with Barcelona's Modernist movement at the end of the nineteenth century, and landmark colorful and ornate buildings are sprinkled throughout the district and are a testament to the geniuses of the era: Lluís Domènech i Montaner, Josep Puig i Cadafalch, and, most famous of all, Antoni Gaudí.

The Spanish civil war from 1936 to 1939 and the subsequent decades of Fascist dictatorship brought devastation to all of Spain. Hundreds of thousands of Spaniards lost their lives, and countless historical buildings and monuments were badly damaged or destroyed. Scars from the war can still be seen in many corners of Barcelona, such as the Gothic Quarter's Plaça Felip Neri, where shrapnel marks from a bomb remain sharply impaled in walls of the square's baroque church.

After the death of dictator General Franco in 1975, Catalan citizens, whose culture and language had been repressed for more than forty years, began to quietly reclaim their heritage by erecting monuments to leaders of the struggle for Catalan independence and changing street names from the state-imposed Castillian to their original Catalan.

Barcelona underwent yet another extensive renovation when it was chosen to host the Olympic Games in the summer of 1992. The city rebuilt and enhanced everything from the mountains to the sea, creating state-of-the art stadiums on Montjuic and developing the city's coast to offer beautiful beaches, marinas, and many other facilities. When the eyes of the world were upon Barcelona in 1992, they saw one of the most exciting and innovative cities in the world, renowned for its dazzling architecture, cutting-edge restaurants and clubs, and countless cultural events.

Geographically, residents are right to point out how spoiled they are by Barcelona's prime location on the Mediterranean. Buffered by the smooth sea, residents are blessed by a temperate climate that enjoys a breeze off the water and is protected from the north winds by the picturesque Collserola hills.

Everything about the city of Barcelona awakens the senses. It captures the essence of the Mediterranean with the striking blue sea, spirited residents, palm trees, and brilliant mosaics. It also epitomizes the best of the modern, fashionable Europe of the future with trendy boutiques and innovative transportation and design. The city is filled with the color and magnificence of the buildings, the sounds of the sea and the people, and the smells of street cafés, bakeries, and exotic gourmet tapas. The dizzying combination of Barcelona's diverse charms makes it a city that is difficult for visitors to leave and easy for them to return to.

Saint James Square stands at the meeting point of the two main streets of ancient Roman Barcelona and now joins principal streets carrer Ferran and carrer Jaume I in the center of the Gothic Quarter. Plaça St. Jaume is home to Barcelona's city hall on the opposite side of the square and the Palau de la Generalitat, or Autonomous Government of Catalonia Palace, pictured here in 1915. Built in the fifteenth century and formerly known as Palau de la Diputació, the palace underwent extensive renovation in 1823, long before this picture was taken.

The Palau de la Generalitat now bears both the Spanish national flag and the striped regional flag of Catalonia. Plaça St. Jaume has been at the center of many key historical events, such as the proclamation of the Catalan state in 1931, the return from a thirty-eight-year exile of politician Josep Tarradellas in 1977 (to instigate the re-creation of an autonomous government for Catalonia), and the celebration of the championship soccer titles of F.C. Barcelona with its fans crowded in the square. The building is open to the public every Sunday, as well as on Saint George's Day, April 23.

Plaça Nova, shown here in a photograph taken in 1942, was initially a small clearing just outside the gates to the Roman city. From 1355 to 1358 this small and unassuming space underwent some construction and was made into an official square in the heart of the Gothic Quarter next to the city's cathedral. The two towers are originally Roman and were extensively restored in the twelfth century. In the sixteenth century various windows were installed in the imposing towers.

In 1991 a project was begun to open up this plaza to the adjacent cathedral and combine the Pla de la Seu (Clearing of the Cathedral) and Plaça Nova to create one large, modern plaza in front of the monument. The two Roman towers were carefully preserved, although the blocks of apartment buildings attached to the left tower have been demolished. The towers, which stood grandly in the diminutive Plaça Nova, are now somewhat dwarfed by the spires of the cathedral (not shown), which reach as high as 230 feet. The figure of Saint Roc watches over the modernized plaza from his glass-encased perch inside the tower at left.

Plaça del Rei, or King's Square, once the central courtyard of the royal palace of the counts of Barcelona, is hidden behind the apse of the cathedral in the Gothic Quarter. The freestanding column is a remnant from the Roman times when Barcelona, or Barcino, was a recently founded Roman city. The stairs behind the column lead to the Saló del Tinell, the main hall of this fourteenth-century palace, where meetings of the infamous Spanish Inquisition were held. Columbus was received here by Ferdinand and Isabella after his 1492 voyage. In the center of the photo, the Renaissance rectangular tower, Torre del Rei Marti, rises above the plaza. On the right is the fourteenth-century Capella de Santa Agueda, or St. Agatha's Chapel, and the building on the left is the Palau del Lloctinent, the sixteenth-century viceroy's palace.

While the square from this angle appears much the same as it did at the time of the earlier photograph, there have been some fascinating new additions in the twentieth century that have all taken place underground. The Casa Clariana Padellàs, just in front of the square, was originally located nearby at Mercaders Street and was moved brick by brick to the Plaça del Rei before the demolition of the area to open up new spaces in the old town. As soon as excavation started, workers discovered a treasure trove of old Barcino, with discernible ruins of streets, homes, and even wineries with preserved mosaic flooring. The entire area has been impeccably preserved and stands under the plaza as the central exhibit in the History Museum. The Roman column is also gone from the square, returned to its original location in the nearby Roman Temple of Augustus.

Barcelona's Gothic Quarter is a labyrinth of narrow pedestrian streets, most of which are centuries old. Carrer Bisbe, or Bishop Street, dates back to when the Romans founded Barcelona—then known as Barcino—between 15 and 10 BC. In Roman times the street was a main thoroughfare known as Decumanus. The Palau de la Generalitat, pictured here, has been in existence and housed Catalonia's government since the Middle Ages. The palace has undergone many renovations and expansions over the years.

The visible portion of the street remains unchanged with one important exception: the intricate bridge overhead that joins the Palau de la Generalitat and the Canons' Houses, the official residence of the Catalan president. The bridge is deceptive because its Gothic style integrates perfectly with the surrounding neighborhood and the nearby cathedral, yet it was actually built in 1928 by Joan Rubió i Bellver. Rubió i Bellver, a disciple of Antoni Gaudí's, belonged to the end of the Modernist or Art Nouveau movement. The neighborhood that houses the Carrer Bisbe is popular with visitors and young locals. It has become a place of great contrasts. Often there are harpists and guitarists playing traditional songs, contributing to the historical atmosphere of the Gothic neighborhood, while businesses range from traditional craftsmen to young fashion designers and upscale restaurants.

The original temple of Santa Maria del Pi, photographed here in 1932, was built between 1319 and 1391. The architectural style is pure Gothic, with a solitary nave and smaller, almost unadorned side chapels. The main façade is dominated by a large, rose stained-glass window, emblematic of the style of Gothic churches of the era. The name of the church and the square—Plaça del Pi—originates from the fact that a small pine tree has stood in the same location since the beginning of the plaza's recorded history. In the distant past, when the square doubled as a cemetery, the pine tree was accompanied by cyprus trees.

In 1936, during the Spanish civil war, a great fire destroyed the church's characteristic rose window. It was completely reconstructed and restored to its formidable original size in 1940. The current version of the ever-present pine tree, considerably larger than its predecessor, was planted in 1985. On weekends the bustling plaza is converted into a small market where vendors sell local produce such as olives, cheese, and honey, as well as seasonal decorations at Christmastime. An art market is also held nearby, where local painters display and sell their work—which often consists of reproductions of Santa Maria's impressive and colorful window.

This plaza, tucked away in the heart of the Gothic Quarter, was named for the Italian Jesuit Sant Felip Neri (1515–95). Photographed here in 1916, the church that bears his name and dominates the small square was built in 1752 in the Baroque style. The door of the temple is flanked by two street lamps. The peaceful Sant Felip Neri Square has been built over what was once the cemetery of Montjuic del Bisbe, just at the entrance of the medieval Jewish Quarter of Barcelona, commonly called Call.

The plaza remains a quiet and solemn spot, but with one especially dramatic moment in its history: on January 30, 1938, more than twenty small children who had taken refuge here lost their lives. The front of the church is scarred by the shrapnel from a severe bombing raid that destroyed the façade of the church. The façade remains unrepaired and serves as a reminder of the horrors of the civil war. Lamps hang from the church façade now and a fountain in the middle of the square creates an oasis of peace just feet away from the bustle of the streets that surround Barcelona's cathedral.

This view of Barcelona from the Montjuic cable car is a good benchmark to show the development of the city in the intervening years and also the relationship between some of its principal landmarks. The Columbus Statue dominates the foreground, with the Port Building to its right on the sea front. Leading away from the great statue is the tree-lined boulevard La Rambla, while Barcelona Cathedral is visible to the right, towering above the surrounding apartment buildings. At far right and farther up the hill, the Sagrada Familia is still in its first phase of construction. The Montjuic cable car was opened in 1931 and it links the city with the hill of Montjuic, which literally translated means Hill of Jews. In previous centuries, there was a Jewish cemetery on Montjuic.

Eighty years later and the canvas of the city has not changed dramatically. Though the cruise liner is gone, there is now a covered walkway in place to aid passengers disembarking from visiting ships. There has been little encroachment around the Cathedral of modern high-rises and the Sagrada Familia has risen substantially higher, though it is still a long way away from its completion date. The cable car was closed for repair throughout 2005 and reopened for business in 2006. A ride up to Montjuic to see the castle, Palau Nacional, Olympic sites, and gain the best views of Barcelona is an essential part of any tourist's visit to the city.

Built in 1907 and pictured here in 1913, the Port Building was originally used for the bureaucratic processing of passengers arriving in Barcelona from ships docked in the port; it also served as a customs house and post office. The second floor of the building was home to the famous restaurant and resting spot for weary travelers called El Mundial. It was modeled on typical French casinos of the time with four towers, one on each corner of the rectangular frame. Rides on the boats—called *golondrinas*—have been available to tourists since January 1884. The original golondrinas took passengers on a trip from the port to the neighborhood of Barceloneta. The price for the trip was fifteen cents, or one real.

The Port Building was badly damaged during the Spanish civil war and was almost completely rebuilt in 1940. At present its sole occupants are employees of the offices of the port. The golondrina rides are still very popular with tourists. The present-day models are nearly identical to their predecessors, measuring fifty-two feet long by nineteen feet wide and with a capacity for 150 passengers. On the right-hand side of the picture, a small portion of a wooden arch is visible. This is the pier, leading out to an extensive complex built for the 1992 Olympics known as Maremagnum, which houses nightclubs, seafood restaurants, and shops.

Until the expansion of 1850, this old neighborhood was not only a treasure trove of elegant Gothic masterpieces and Roman ruins but a small and densely populated city where residents lived in extremely close quarters between the city's old walls—and in some cases, on top of the walls themselves. This street in the Gothic neighborhood was once home to Barcelona's cobblers. The name "tapineria" originates from the peculiar sandals made of cork, lined with leather, and covered with cloth that were popular with women from the Middle Ages on. Visible in this photo from the early twentieth century are old apartments attached to and almost completely obscuring the Roman wall. Behind the wall is the tower of the Gothic chapel of St. Agata.

Tapineria Street has been cleared to make way for Plaça Ramón Berenguer. The clearing of the apartment blocks attached to the wall began in 1927 by city hall, was interrupted by the Spanish civil war from 1934 to 1939, and was not finished until 1950. In this unusual instance, damage caused by the bombing campaigns during the war was actually useful to the architects and planners, as they helped speed along the planned demolition. The plaza is named for Ramón Berenguer III, Count of Barcelona in the eleventh and twelfth centuries, whose equestrian statue, created by the nineteenth-century sculptor Llimona, was placed in front of the plaza at its inauguration on March 11, 1950.

The main street of Via Laietana was part of a large urban project to open up the narrow maze of streets composing the Gothic Quarter and create a wide path connecting the Eixample neighborhood to the port. It was carried out with great success in 1907, although the extensive construction destroyed more than 2,000 apartment buildings and left 10,000 residents homeless and without any formal relocation plan. The building on the left was the Caïxa de Pensions i d'Estalvis de Barcelona. It was built in neo-Medieval style by Enric Sagnier in 1917 and features a sculpture by Manuel Fuxà depicting an allegory of savings. The office building on the right was also designed by Sagnier, as an annex to the Caixa de Pensions. In this building Sagnier used a completely different and more modern design, and the office block was built with white stone adorned with glazed tiles.

Some have argued that the Gothic Quarter was opened up by Via Laietana and given a breath of fresh air only to be choked instead by the carbon monoxide generated by vehicles on this well-traveled street. Caixa de Pensions remains architecturally intact but is now the home of the Superior Justice court of Catalonia and remains one of the most remarkable buildings in the area. The Annex to the Caixa is of interest mainly because of the similarity between this century-old office space, which was one of the first modern blocks of its kind, and the other more modern office buildings that now surround it.

This photo from around 1930 shows a typical square in the Gothic neighborhood of Via Laietana. The square was named for the statue of an angel placed in front of the old Roman wall of the city. The 1618 statue, now in the Museum of History, is the image of Saint Eulàlia. According to legend, Saint Eulàlia was a young girl living in nearby Sarría around the third century, a time of persecution for Christians under Emperor Diocleciano. She confessed to being a Christian and was submitted to brutal torture and eventual crucifixion in the square. Saint Eulàlia is co-patron saint of Barcelona and is now patron saint of the cathedral of Barcelona, which stands behind the plaza. Her remains are thought to be buried in the crypt under the high altar. In the center of the plaza is the entrance to the newly opened underground metro.

The metro still lies underneath the plaza, which has been opened up by the urban landscaping project of Via Laietana, the busy street behind the plaza that now runs through the Gothic Quarter, connecting the Eixample neighborhood to the port. On Via Laietana, to the right, one can see the emblematic red sign of the CC.OO. or Comisiones Obreras, the most powerful workers' union in Catalonia, with its headquarters here on Via Laietana for more than forty years.

The Palau de la Música is a breathtaking example of Modernist architecture at its full potential. Depicted here is only one small corner of the building that embodies the sculpture, design, and culture of the time, and crowned the end of the Modernist era in Barcelona. The Music Palace was commissioned by Orfeó Català and work was overseen by Lluís Domènech i Montaner. Construction began in 1905 and ended three years later. The concert hall was intended to be the home of Catalan chamber music. The small space available (the site of a former convent), narrow streets, and high price of land resulted in a detail-rich, extremely compact structure that lacks a vantage point from which it can be fully appreciated. The sculpture shown here, by Miquel Blay, is titled *La cancó popular* and depicts Saint George protecting the common people and proudly waving the Catalan flag. It is intended to symbolize the accessibility of Catalan music to the general public, which was the original purpose of the Palau de la Música.

Seen in color, the Palau de la Música appears even more vibrant than when it was first inaugurated. What is not apparent from the photograph is that the Palau narrowly escaped demolition in the 1920s. With Modernism having fallen out of favor, many architects and local residents considered the busy façade an eyesore and lobbied enthusiastically to have it torn down. Fortunately they were unsuccessful, and the concert hall has been in use since its opening. Recently Catalonian architect Oscar Tusquets completed his renovation and extension of the Palau, including the addition of a smaller concert hall with capacity for six hundred people. In 1997 it was declared a World Heritage Site by UNESCO.

The Pla de Palau, or Palace Square, is located close to the waterfront and marks the border between the Ribera and Barceloneta districts. It is named for this grand fifteenth-century medieval structure. Pictured here in the 1870s, the palace, originally known as Halla dels Draps, was built as a textile market. It was a commercial building until it was confiscated in 1654 by King Philip IV for use as a residence by the viceroy. In the nineteenth century, on the occasion of Isabel II's journey to Spain, the palace was ceded to the queen and then underwent extensive reformations to be transformed into the royal residence in Barcelona. There was some controversy when the first Republic of Spain sold the palace in a public auction.

The controversy over the public sale of the royal palace never came to a head, because the entire building was engulfed in flames and burned to the ground on Christmas Day 1875. Apartment buildings with shops, banks, and restaurants on the ground floor now occupy the spot where the palace and

textile market once stood. The street still bears the name Pla de Palau, but the once-somber and regal square has been transformed into a pleasant plaza with a kiosk and playground in the center.

Santa Maria del Mar, built between 1302 and 1350, is considered to be one of the finest examples of Catalan Gothic architecture. This picture shows the rear façade sometime between 1905 to 1915. The food stalls jutting out from the church walls are explained by the proximity to Mercat del Born, Barcelona's central food market at the time. The bridge at left connected a palace with a box in the interior of Santa Maria del Mar, and was constructed for the convenience of Barcelona's royalty and nobility, allowing them to attend religious services without having to suffer the indignity of stepping outside the palace and entering the church through the front door as the common people did.

The food stalls disappeared from the perimeter of the church, as did many grocery stores in this district when the Mercat del Born closed in 1971 and the food market was moved to a newer facility in the suburbs. The bridge—always considered a symbol of political oppression—was also finally dismantled in 1987 and the neighboring buildings were torn down to create space for a new square designed by municipal architect Carme Fiol and inaugurated on

September 11, 1989. September 11 is a public holiday celebrating the formerly repressed Catalan identity, honoring those who defended Barcelona in the 1714 War of the Spanish Succession and were buried in the Cemetery of the Mulberry Trees. The site of this cemetery is now marked by a red, flame-holding arch, visible at left in this picture.

The recorded history of this location in the Ribera neighborhood begins before 1714, when Barcelona was a city that had been recently conquered by the troops of Philip V. He converted the site into a military fortress and relocated its residents to the shorefront area that would later be known as Barceloneta, or "little Barcelona." Almost two centuries after its abandonment, the site was transformed into a busy marketplace, pictured here between 1915 and 1925. The Mercat del Born is a classic example of the iron architecture of the period. Built by Josep Fontseré i Mestre in 1876, it was a center of commercial activity in the neighborhood until 1971 when a new facility, Mercabarna, opened.

The market stood unused for thirty years until February 2002, when the city, with the enthusiastic support of local residents, began a project to convert the building into a public library. At the start of construction, however, workers discovered centuries-old ruins beneath the foundation of the marketplace. A great debate ensued, pitting the historians and archaeologists, who argued the importance of preserving this remarkable old underground city, against residents of the neighborhood, who preferred to have a good public library in a city already rich with museums and historic sites. In the end the historians and architects prevailed, and the ruins will be conserved while plans for the library have been postponed.

A. T. V. — 41 - BARCELONA
Entrada del Parque

This photograph, taken between 1905 and 1915, depicts the two statues that flank this entrance of the Parc de la Ciutadella, placed at the intersection of Avinguda del Marques de l'Argentera and Passeig Picasso in the year 1884. The statue on the left symbolizes agriculture with its wheat ears, grape bunches, and fruits, and the other is an allegory of the navy, with such distinctive elements as an anchor and chains tied up to moorings. Some nineteenth-century critics questioned the artistic quality of these sculptures by Venanci Vallmitjana and wondered what the relation between the navy and a landlocked public garden could possibly be.

The sculptures underwent a thorough restoration in the year 2001, and although the streets have been paved and equipped with traffic lights, and cars rather than horses can enter the park, this modern view shows virtually the same image as before. Clearly visible here are the pedestals on which the statues stand, which reportedly were conceived by Antoni Gaudí. These two statues have counterparts at the other entrance of the park that are allegories of commerce and industry and built by Agapit Vallmitjana, Venanci's brother.

This image from the early 1930s shows a distinctive building of unpainted brick known as Castell dels Tres Dragons, or Three Dragon Castle. It was built at the entrance to Ciutadella Park by the great Modernist architect Lluís Domènech i Montaner in 1887 to serve as the café and restaurant for the 1888 Universal Exposition. Both the exposed brick and the iron structures were radical architectural innovations at the time. For the first time, brick was used as a decorative material instead of a mere construction element. The building later became the site of an important workshop where Modernist artists met to study ceramics and forged iron techniques.

The Castle of the Three Dragons now houses the Zoology Museum and welcomes visitors to its beautiful corner location at the entrance of Barcelona's Parc de la Ciutadella. The Zoology museum—which, together with the Geology Museum forms the Natural Science Museum—houses the zoology collections and permanent exhibitions as well as temporary exhibition rooms of the Natural Science Museum. Greeting visitors is the skeleton of a whale—there is no trace of any dragon.

This structure, known as "the waterfall," in the center of the city park Ciutadella, began as a modest project, but as it was constructed it grew to be the ornate structure pictured here in the 1920s. Construction started on the fountain in 1875 and it was finally inaugurated in June 1881. Architect Josep Fontseré i Mestre was helped by his then-apprentice and now Modernist legend, Antoni Gaudí. The fountain is surrounded by a large staircase and culminates in a sculpture representing the chariot of Aurora. The upper part is a grotto featuring large stalactites. At its inauguration, the waterfall was criticized for being very costly and out of place in the middle of a flat park.

The fountain, like much of Barcelona, was completely restored in 1992 and is now an integral part of the Ciutadella park, surrounded by gardens designed to showcase it and the surrounding monuments. This is a great picnic area where families gather together on weekends after visiting Barcelona's zoo, which is located inside the same park.

Sculptor Torquat Tasso won a competition sponsored by the city hall of Barcelona to create this bronze statue of famed eighteenth-century Catalan painter Antoni Viladomat. It was completed in May 1888 for the Universal Exposition and pictured here in 1905. The statue was part of a series of eight monuments dedicated to great Catalan thinkers and artists of the eighteenth century and stands on the street that was then known as Salo de Sant Joan. Tasso's intention was to portray Viladomat's likeness as well as his work as an academic, a man whose art was worthy of regard equal to his contributions to science and literature.

The aging but regal sculpture still exists on the street now known as Passeig Lluís Companys, named for the former president of Catalonia and defender of Catalan independence, who was executed for political reasons during the dictatorship of General Franco. The background view of the Arc de Triomf is obscured by the tall, stately palm trees that now line the paved street. On the right-hand side one can catch a glimpse of an original Modernist-style street lamp designed by Pere Falqués i Urpí. Up until the civil war the street boasted a total of eight statues of main figures in Catalan history, but at present, that of Viladomat and one other of Roger de Llúria, the well-known Catalan navigator, are all that remain.

Barcelona's one-hundred-foot-high Arc de Triomf was built by architect Josep Vilaseca i Casanovas to serve as the main entrance gate to the 1888 Universal Exposition. Legend has it that Vilaseca i Casanovas was afraid the monument would collapse when the scaffolding was taken off, which fortunately didn't happen. The triumph of progress—rather than military dominance—was the idea that inspired Barcelona's Arc de Triomf and differentiates it from other similar European monuments such as the Arc de Triomphe in Paris. The monument is adorned with sculptures and a coat of arms representing all of the Spanish provinces, with Barcelona in the center.

The structure of the Arc de Triomf is very well preserved, and Vilaseca i Casanovas would be pleasantly surprised to find his monument remarkably sound and virtually unchanged after more than a century. It underwent restoration in 1989 and continues to attract visitors, as well as locals, who gather in the plaza on summer evenings to watch the free movies that are projected on a screen erected just behind the building. Palm trees have been planted and new apartment buildings occupy the neighboring plots.

Carrer Ferran begins at La Rambla and runs north to Plaça de Sant Jaume, connecting two main landmarks in the old town. The street was first built in 1827 and named carrer Ferran VII to mark the occasion of the visit paid by the monarch, King Ferran VII of Spain, that year. At the time the picture was taken, in the 1880s, the streets around carrer Ferran VII still housed the apartments of the city's upper classes as well as the offices of liberal professionals such as doctors and lawyers, all of whom would soon move uptown to the developing Eixample district. In 1910, and not without heated debate, the city hall changed the street's name to simply "carrer Ferran," thereby avoiding a specific reference to the last absolutist king in the history of Spain.

The location of the street in the heart of Barcelona has kept it a busy artery over the years but the atmosphere and the type of businesses have changed dramatically in the last decades. Today this is a thriving tourist district, and Irish pubs abound on carrer Ferran and the entrance at La Rambla is flanked by two international fast food chains. Some of the old charm is maintained in the architectural details, such as the beautiful street lamps that replaced the ones shown on the previous page and on some intricate and colorful Modernist-style storefronts. The lights were designed by the talented Catalan architect Josep Maria Jujol in 1902.

As you look down the central boulevard known as La Rambla, vendors, artists, and other people merge in a busy street scene. Each part of La Rambla goes by a different name. Traditionally La Rambla de Sant Josep, shown here, is called Rambla de les Flors, because of the many flower stalls that flank this boulevard. The history of the flower market is similar to that of the neighboring Boqueria Market: originally the vendors would arrive and set up their stalls each day, but since 1853 there have been permanent flower kiosks. The first attempts to create a unified design for the different stands date to 1869, and this picture, taken in 1915, reflects the changes introduced in 1888 for the Universal Exposition.

Fortunately, some things haven't changed much, and the essential ingredients of this charming section of La Rambla remain the same; the traditional vendors, florists, and artists persist and are admired every day by locals and an increasing number of international tourists. It is impossible to stroll down La Rambla today without noticing the beautiful flowers that adorn both sides of the central aisle, near the market entrance. Roses, carnations, freesias, and orchids fill the air with the aroma of spring every day of the year. The design of the current stalls dates from the 1990s.

The bustling Boqueria market, shown here around 1910, is believed to have its origins in medieval times as an open-air itinerant merchants' market. The first mention of commercial activities in the area is a 1217 reference to the buying and selling of meat. Nearby St. Joseph's convent stood on the site for centuries but burned down in 1835. After the convent's demolition, the wandering vendors quickly took over the prime location between the pedestrian street of La Rambla and the old city wall, and soon the first permanent structure to house the market was inaugurated. However, large portions of the market were still "unofficial" and stands for the florists, fruit sellers, fishmongers, and butchers were built bit by bit throughout the nineteenth century. Roofing and additional permanent stalls were added in 1914, and the market remained virtually untouched by renovation and expansion until 2001.

The Boqueria market as it stands today is the largest in Spain. It attracts tourists who come to see the Modernist stained-glass entrance and marvel at the variety of goods, which includes everything from fish, meat, and seafood to spices and exotic insects. It also remains a popular market with locals who still have the custom of doing their daily shopping and chatting with the vendors about which is the best cut of pork for roasting or how to sauté wild mushrooms. The long-overdue restoration in 2001 by architects Lluís Clotet and Ignacio Paricio opened it up to La Rambla, creating a high roof, bringing in more light, and exposing the Ionic columns within.

The Gran Teatre del Liceu has witnessed many happy and tragic episodes from its privileged location on the central part of the vibrant Rambla. The opera house/theater was only forty years old when this picture was taken in the 1880s, but it had already been reconstructed after a fire completely destroyed the hall and the stage in April 1861. The theater at the time was considered a symbol of the city's oligarchic upper classes and soon became a target for anarchists. In 1893 a bomb exploded, causing twenty fatalities. By contrast, the end of the nineteenth century also saw inspirational moments, such as the appearance of the much-applauded Richard Wagner in 1883.

The façade doesn't quite reflect the dramatic changes the Teatre del Liceu has undergone in the last years. On January 31, 1994, yet another fire destroyed much of the opera house, which had a major impact on Catalan society, as people came to terms with the fact that flames had once again devoured this cultural symbol in the heart of Barcelona. Amid much controversy, in 1999 the Teatre del Liceu was rebuilt and enlarged over the adjoining sites on La Rambla and opened for the third time in its turbulent history. Efforts have been made to make the theater less elitist and more accessible to the general public.

This unusual picture from 1880 shows the Plaça Reial, or Royal Square, covered in snow—a rare occurrence given the mild climate of Barcelona. The square was built in 1848, right off La Rambla, on the site of a former convent that had been destroyed following the 1835 Mendizábal laws that confiscated the church properties. The square is formed by arcaded buildings containing large, luxurious residences for Barcelona's upper classes. It is linked with the adjoining streets by means of alleys such as Passatge Bacardi and Passatge Madoz. In the middle of the square stands the Fountain of Three Graces. The Modernist lampposts were designed by a very young Antoni Gaudí in 1878.

In the twentieth century the square went through a squalid period of decline. The residences were abandoned and the formerly "royal" plaza became a center of drug dealing, thievery, and prostitution. In the past few decades the square has been revived and reinvented as a lively tourist spot. It was closed to automobile traffic, the smaller trees were replaced by tall, stately palm trees, and the ground floors now house cafés, bars, and nightclubs. The upper floors are still home to a few residents as well as a number of budget hostels for young international travelers. Once a week coin collectors gather to trade and sell their wares at an open-air market.

Perhaps the most famous part of Barcelona, La Rambla is a mile-long pedestrian boulevard that stretches from central Plaza Catalunya down to the port. The name Rambla comes from the Arabic for "stream." The original Rambla was a small stream outside the walls of the city. In the sixteenth century, a university and some convents were built along the stream, and when the bulk of the city wall was torn down in the nineteenth century, development of the area began in earnest. La Rambla is divided into five sections: the Ramblas de Canaletes (or Rambla of the Fountain), dels Estudis (named for sixteenth-century university Estudis Generals, which was demolished in 1843), de Sant Josep (named after the convent of St. Joseph, which burned down in the 1800s and upon whose original site stands the famous Boqueria market), dels Caputxins, and de Santa Mónica (named after a convent at the end of La Rambla).

La Rambla is more vibrant than ever. Tourists and locals flock to this area at all hours of the day and night. Lined with kiosks open until the small hours; cafés serving sangria, beer, and coffee; flower stalls; and even pet sellers with tanks and cages of birds, lizards, rabbits, and snakes, La Rambla is a strange mix of the traditional and the curious. In the twentieth century La Rambla became famous for its human statues: people in makeup and costume dressed, for example, as native Americans or bronze statues, who remain perfectly still until a coin is dropped into the contribution jar—then they spring to life. On the downside, with the surge of international tourism in Barcelona in recent years, La Rambla is also famous for its extremely skilled pickpockets.

The eighteen-inch finger of Christopher Columbus has been pointing eastward toward the Indies for a long time now. In 1881 the city hall decided that Barcelona should have a monument dedicated to the discoverer of America and a year later a jury finally selected the project presented by Gaietà Buigas i Monravà. The government donated thirty tons of bronze from obsolete weaponry and military equipment for the purpose of building the statue. The construction lasted for seven years and required the excavation of seventeen-foot-deep foundations. The transportation of the pieces of the statue on multiple horse carriages from the workshop in the old town and their assembly at its site on Portal de la Pau was an ambitious and complicated project. This picture was taken in 1887, when the statue was almost ready for its inauguration the following year.

Columbus continues to keep watch over the ships arriving at the Barcelona harbor and dominates the skyline of Barcelona from his position 196 feet up, but he is no longer the young man he was back in the nineteenth century, despite four "facelifts," in 1929, 1965, 1976, and 1985. Today, the monument attracts many visitors. Some pose on the lions at the base for a souvenir photo of the city and others venture inside the column to take the inner elevator all the way up to the orb under Columbus's feet for one of the best aerial views of La Rambla and the Gothic Quarter.

Barceloneta, or "little Barcelona," is a small triangular peninsula that juts out into the Mediterranean Sea from the Gothic Quarter. Traditionally the district has been home to working-class citizens with close ties to the sea that surrounds them; men who weren't fishermen often worked as longshoremen or building ships, and women often sold the day's catch in front of their modest apartment buildings. This image from between 1910 and 1920 shows a group of fishermen fixing their nets and preparing them for the next day in the last light from the afternoon sun. In the background, the hill of Montjuic dominates the harbor.

Fishing is no longer a way of life in the city of Barcelona, and the boats in present-day Port Vell are more likely to be privately owned yachts, hire boats, floating bars, or nightclubs. While the neighborhood is no longer famous for its fishermen, the marine tradition lives on in the numerous excellent seafood restaurants and tapas bars that line the narrow city streets. The white cube-shaped building in the background is the IMAX cinema, constructed as part of the port's commercial development, which includes a state-of-the-art aquarium and an entertainment complex built just before the 1992 Olympic Games. Every year Port Vell is visited by more than sixteen million people.

This Gothic monument was built more than seven hundred years ago as a dockyard for the construction, maintenance, and repair of ships coming into the port of Barcelona, as well as for winter storage. It was used as the royal shipyard until 1745. At the time this picture was taken, between 1930 and 1932, the military used the space as an arsenal for artillery pieces and tanks.

The city expansion project—or Cerdà Plan of 1859—included plans to demolish the building to make way for a road to join the new Eixample neighborhood with the port, but owing to a campaign by historian Carreras Candi and support from the military population, the building escaped demolition and was finally returned to the city by the military in 1929.

In 1936, during the Spanish civil war, the evacuation of soldiers left the arsenal free for other uses, and it was slated to become the Museu Marítim de Catalunya (Catalonia Maritime Museum). The total area of the building was expanded from 43,056 square feet in 1941 to 108,000 square feet in 1985 to accommodate the museum, and in the same year architects Esteve and

Robert Terrades drew up grand plans to transform the museum into a benchmark area for the promotion of maritime culture and history. The future of the Maritime Museum was ensured in 1993 when it received substantial funding for development and conservation from the city of Barcelona and the Port Authorities.

Near the end of the main street leading to the port is the grand Porta de Santa Madrona. This is the last well-preserved piece of the fortresslike wall built in the fifteenth century to protect the city. Pictured here is the main entrance gate, still in use at the time of this photograph in 1910. The gate was previously known as Dreçana and was later named after Saint Madrona.

The lower part of the tower was reconstructed in 1664. At the time, the gate was of such importance that any modifications had to be approved by the crown, and later, by the city council as well. Pieces of the wall were damaged during the urban reforms of the mid-nineteenth century.

The gate, built to dissuade invading troops and protect the citizens of Barcelona, still stands centuries later as an imposing remnant of the mighty fortress it once was. The upper part of the towers has been restored and a protective wall was built around the base to discourage vandalism. The Porta de Santa Madrona is very close to La Rambla and many buses park here to load and unload tourists seeking to explore the old town.

Avinguda Parallel was opened to the public on October 8, 1894. The avenue runs diagonally from Plaza España to the port and the street is not actually parallel to any other in Barcelona. Its name originates from the fact that its path coincides with the longitudinal parallel 41°22′34″ North. This neighborhood was traditionally the old theater district. The avenue was lined with nightclubs, cabarets, and Bohemian cafés. It was home to El Molino,

Barcelona's small replica of the famous Parisian Moulin Rouge, and the Theatre Arnau, visible on the right side of the photograph. In 1911, just two years before this picture was taken, the Arnau had the honor of hosting the debut of Raquel Meller, who went on to become the grand dame of Spanish theater in the 1920s and '30s.

Parallel is now a main artery of the city, congested with cars and buses. The cobblestones and the magic of the theater have all but disappeared. Only three theaters remain open: the Victòria, the Apolo, and the Condal, and repeated attempts to revitalize the now-abandoned El Molino have thus far been unsuccessful. On the right side of the photo, behind the trees, is the defunct Teatro Arnau. In the small square in front of the theater, to the right of the bus stop, is a fountain with a statue dedicated to the once-great and now almost-forgotten Raquel Meller.

Looking south in this 1860s photograph, one sees the old *muralla de mar*, or sea wall. The sea wall was first erected in the sixteenth century to protect the city against naval attacks, and by the nineteenth century it had turned into a popular promenade for the upper-class inhabitants of Barcelona because of its splendid view of the harbor and its proximity to the old city center. The sea wall was torn down in 1868.

The area has evolved into the palm tree–lined Passeig Colom. The first major transformation of this neighborhood commenced with the disappearance of the sea wall in 1868. The area, like so many in Barcelona, was further developed for the 1888 Universal Exposition in Barcelona. The area was also redeveloped between 1983 and 1987 by Manuel de Solá-Morales when the warehouses of the industrial port were moved farther down the coastline. In the distance is the monument to Columbus, erected in 1888.

This whimsical gate marks the entrance to the Park Güell, constructed in 1900 and named after Eusebi Güell, who commissioned Antoni Gaudí to bring to life his vision of a landscape that was part real estate investment, part ecological project, and part artistic utopia. Güell envisioned a gated "garden city" with his thirty-seven-acre property carved up into sixty plots of land and strict regulations that would force buyers to build houses in keeping with the aesthetic of the park. The land was largely devoid of plant life, so he arranged for gardens to be created based on Mediterranean species, which are stronger and require less water and maintenance than more fashionable English gardens. Shown at this entrance is the rubble-work wall that surrounds the park and is adorned with colorful mosaics made of broken pieces of tile scavenged from factory waste.

In the end, only three of the sixty plots of land were sold. One of these was the show home, which was purchased by Gaudí himself in 1906 and is now a museum dedicated to his work and life. The park's entrance now boasts an iron door emblazoned with the words "Park Güell" in typical mosaic motif. The grilles for the door were added in 1965 and came from one of Gaudí's

buildings that was undergoing repair. Following the death of Eusebi Güell in 1918, Park Güell opened to the public in 1922. In 1969, amid negotiations for the construction of a large hotel on the site, the park was declared a national monument to avoid its commercialization. The park has been undergoing a slow and painstaking restoration since 1985.

Barceloneta is a peninsula that juts out of the port of the city, almost in the shape of a flag. The neighborhood was erected in the eighteenth century when plans were made for creating the Ciutadella fortress. Fishermen, factory workers, and other blue-collar families were uprooted from their homes on the site of the future park and moved to Barceloneta. At the time of this photograph, Barcelona was not considered a city on the sea; the small and neglected Port Vell was almost exclusively for industrial use. The exception to the rule was the neighborhood of Barceloneta, which by the early twentieth century had a well-established maritime tradition and whose residents considered themselves a separate entity from the residents of "mainland" Barcelona. In summer Barcelonans flocked to Barceloneta to enjoy the sea. Pictured here are the changing tents on the shores of the Barceloneta beach.

One of the most radical changes brought by the 1992 Olympic Games was the embracing of the sea by the city of Barcelona. Before the summer games there was a massive cleanup of the Barcelona shoreline and new, artificial beaches were created from imported sand on both sides of what became the Olympic Village. These included the beach of Barceloneta, which has become a top tourist destination due to the variety of traditional seafood restaurants sprinkled along the shore and in the narrow streets. The beach has been widened and given a wooden promenade. The two towers in the distance mark the site of the Olympic Village, which still holds a luxury hotel, a casino, and various upscale restaurants. Also visible is the giant bronze whale sculpture by Frank Gehry.

Pictured here is the once-notorious Barri de Pekin neighborhood, in the past one of the most depressed districts in the city. Largely populated by fishermen and industrial workers employed by factories behind the shoreline, living conditions were abysmal and families lived in dilapidated tenements or, as pictured, directly on the beach in shacks constructed from cheap materials scavenged from the streets. Overcrowding, flooding, and unsanitary conditions, and homes with neither running water nor electricity were the norm. This picture, taken in the first decade of the twentieth century, shows the damage inflicted on the shanty housing after heavy rains.

This area has a new lease on life thanks to a combination of events. The redevelopment that took place in preparation for the 1992 Olympics has attracted more wealthy Barcelonans to the Mediterranean coast. In the distance one can see that the dilapidated buildings and pollution-producing factories have been replaced by luxury high-rise condominiums with sea views. In the background, at the end of the promenade on the right, is the convention center built for Forum 2004, a widely promoted celebration of cultures and diversity. The citizens of Barcelona continue to enjoy the revived coastline and people flock to the Mediterranean in both the summer and the winter to swim, shop, and fly kites.

Pictured here in 1929 is the Plaça Catalunya in the very center of town above La Rambla. The square was first inaugurated in 1927 for the visit of King Alfonso XIII. The many sculptures that decorate the square were put in place later, before the 1929 exposition. The statue pictured here, *La Deessa* by Clara, was the center of a great controversy brought on by a campaign by moralist groups against the naked sculptures that adorned the plaza. In order to prevent incidents and sabatoge it had to be removed three days after it was initially placed there, and then put back again the night before the inauguration of the exposition. In the background is the Hotel Colon, the most luxurious hotel in the city at the time.

The present statue is a replica created in 1982 to protect the original *La Deessa* from deterioration. The original is now in the reception area of the city hall, on Plaça de Sant Jaume. The replica faces the opposite direction and sits in the middle of a pond. The Hotel Colon has disappeared and an office building occupies its place; the modern plaza is dominated by large bank offices and department stores.

This photograph shows the intersection of main streets Rambla Catalunya and Gran Via in approximately 1915. The monument pictured was unveiled in 1888 and dedicated to Joan Güell, father of Eusebi Güell, who was the mentor of famous architect Antoni Gaudí. Joan Güell was a leading figure of industry and influential politician of the time. The monument was, like so many others in Barcelona, destroyed during the Spanish civil war and rebuilt later, but on a nearby esplanade. In the background at left is Casa Pia Batlló, a Modernist building of 1896.

Instead of the monument to Joan Güell, today there is a whimsical fountain depicting four children riding on top of fish. The fountain was created by wealthy Catalan sculptor Frederic Mares, who donated his house, his large collection of artwork, and artifacts to the city of Barcelona. The collection forms the basis of the Frederic Mares Museum near the city's cathedral. The eye-catching and picturesque fountain was moved here from its original location in Plaça Catalunya in 1961 and has since caused quite a few traffic accidents involving distracted motorists.

March 17, 1938, was a black day in the history of Barcelona. On that day, the city suffered a series of bombings that completely destroyed the corner of two of the city's main streets, Gran Via de les Corts Catalanes and carrer Balmes. Italian air raids hit a truck loaded with explosives, causing the destruction shown in this picture and the deaths of some six hundred people. The Spanish civil war was one of the bloodiest events in the history of Spain. It took place between 1936 and 1939 and finished with the victory of the fascists troops of General Francisco Franco, marking the start of an oppressive dictatorship that lasted until Franco's death in 1975.

Life has returned to this place in the city center. The buildings damaged by the bombs were rebuilt and now throngs of people congregate here to go to the movies at the Cinema Coliseum, the building crowned by two towers in the center of the photo, or to sit on the benches to talk and eat sunflower seeds. In front of the movie theater, a small sculpture dedicated to the victims of all wars is an inconspicuous and indirect reminder of the bombings of 1938. Every day, people passing by stop and look down at the inscription on the ground without being aware of the 1938 bombings that it indirectly commemorates.

This picture from around 1930 shows the U-shaped building of the Universitat de Barcelona. Building started in 1863 in what was then the surrounding countryside, arousing the curiosity of neighboring Barcelonans. This medieval-inspired building was one of the first built outside the recently demolished ancient walls of the city in the Eixample district. Its creation signified the consolidation of the university's historic return to Barcelona from Cervera, where it was moved after Barcelona's defeat in the 1714 War of the Spanish Succession. The university took more than twenty years to complete. At the center of the plaza stands a monument to Doctor Robert, the mayor of Barcelona at the end of the nineteenth century, created by prominent Modernist sculptor Josep Llimona. The university occupies two blocks between Gran Via, Balmes, Diputacio, and Aribau.

The building in Plaça Universitat is still in daily use, its interior gardens and courtyards full of students, and the clock tower marking time. In the mid-twentieth century the university building by Elias Rogent proved too small to house all the different disciplines contained by the Universitat de Barcelona, and to respond to the rapidly growing number of students a new campus was developed in another part of town. What was once on the outskirts of the city has now become part of its large, modern center. The monument to Doctor Robert was taken down for political reasons during the dictatorship following Spain's civil war. It survived its exile, however, and lives on, reerected in Plaça Tetuan on the other side of the city.

The corner where Passeig de Gràcia meets Aragó Street has long been a central point in Barcelona. It has been the headquarters for nearly every type of public transportation used in Barcelona. In 1872 the first tramway system passed through here. Pictured above is the commuter train entrance soon after its inauguration on July 1, 1902. The train station converted this spot into one of the main gateways into Barcelona until 1922, when it was necessary to expand the space to accommodate more travelers and a new building was constructed.

The commuter train system was moved underground in the 1960s and is no longer visible, although it follows the same route more than one hundred years later. Aragó Street continues to be a main transportation artery above-ground and one of the most popular roads used to access the city center. It is now crowded with more modern forms of transportation such as cars, taxis, motorbikes, trucks, and buses. At left, in a prime location, is the retail store Burberry, located in one of the most sought-after buildings in Barcelona. Over the past ten years the building has housed the Fashion Café, a short-lived supermodel-backed restaurant, and a mobile phone company.

Casa Lleo i Morera was constructed in 1902 by architect Lluís Domènech i Montaner. The building was awarded first prize in an architectural competition by the city of Barcelona in 1906. This Modernist jewel is located on the main boulevard Passeig de Gràcia and forms part of the Manzana de la Discordia, a set of several emblematic Modernist buildings located side by side on one block. The original owner was Doctor Lleo i Morera. Lleo means "lion" and Morera means "mulberry," so the architect used his patron's name for inspiration and adorned the façade with lions and mulberries. This picture from 1905 shows the ground floor, with sculptures by Eusebi Arnau jutting out from the façade at the street level.

Casa Lleo i Morera was the victim of an anti-Modernist architecture movement in 1944. The excessive ornamentation and detail-work fell out of fashion in Barcelona, and this style of architecture was dubbed by some art historians of the period as "the epoch of bad taste." The ground floor was acquired by upscale fashion house Loewe, which subsequently funded a complete redesign of the space by Noucentista architect Duran i Reynals, completely changing the appearance of the building. The sculptures by Eusebi Arnau were destroyed. Decades later, amid growing public criticism of the "mutilation" of the original construction, and with Modernism back in favor, architects Óscar Tusquets and Carles Diaz restored the original façade and reconstructed the pinnacle that had formerly crowned the building. In 1988 Casa Lleo i Morera regained its original place as one of the most significant and spectacular examples of Modernist architecture in Barcelona.

In 1898 the building now known as Casa Amatller was an unremarkable structure similar to most others built at the end of the nineteenth century in the expansion neighborhood of Barcelona. It was acquired by the chocolate maker Antoni Amatller, who intended to convert the building into a noteworthy private residence. Amatller, whose name means "almond tree," hired architect Josep Puig i Cadafalch, who carried out extensive remodeling to convert the building into a north European Gothic-style house. The façade, vestibule, and first floor were all transformed into a Modernist masterpiece with ornamental work inspired by almond trees and by Amatller's hobbies of photography and collection of glass art. At the time of the picture, 1905, the business at the street level was an insurance company and the entrance was through a door in the hall of the house.

The structural difference with the previous picture is that a door was opened on the right-hand side of the façade to allow direct access to the street. The insurance company has been replaced by a jewelry shop. After Amatller's death in 1910, his only daughter Teresa Amatller inherited the house and resided there her entire life. Teresa had no heirs, so in order to protect the integrity of the house and the collector's items her family had accrued over the years, she created a foundation called Institut Amatller d'Art Hispanic. Upon her death in 1960 the foundation took over her inheritance and the care of the Amatller family collection. They maintain a library and photograph archive in the building. Some of the apartments in the Casa Amatller are still occupied by residential tenants.

This 1910 picture shows the enigmatic building Antoni Gaudí created for the prominent textile industrialist Josep Batlló in 1906. Gaudí never explained the scheme of the complex façade, but there are several fascinating theories. The most probable, according to experts, is that it is a rendering of the legend of Saint George, patron saint of Catalunya (and England), who slew a dragon to save a princess. The roof would represent the scaly back of the dragon, the cross that crowns the building would be the sword of Saint George, and the menacing balconies could be interpreted as the many bones and skulls of the dragon's victims. Another hypothesis is that the building was meant to be a permanent physical manifestation of carnival celebrations: the roof could be the hat of a harlequin; the balconies, traditional Venetian carnival masks; and the multicolored fragments of ceramics and glass scattered throughout the façade, the confetti thrown by revelers.

Gaudí's colorful and astonishing Casa Batlló has been meticulously maintained, both inside and out. It is privately owned and was closed to the public for decades; however, in 2002 the building was opened to the public in honor of what would have been the architect's 150th birthday. What was meant to be a temporary opening of the building has proven so popular that the owners have decided to continue allowing public visits for the foreseeable future. Now visitors are able to see the equally masterful and complex interior design. The building has also been made available for special events such as weddings and business meetings.

CASA COMALAT

Salvador Valeri

This often-overlooked Modernist building by Salvador Valeri i Pupurull was built between 1909 and 1911 and the picture shown here was taken soon after. Located on the border of the Eixample and Gràcia neighborhoods on Avinguda Diagonal, the building has two distinct façades. The façade pictured here is actually the rear of the building, with a curved design to accommodate the city corner upon which it stands. It features decorations of unusual Modernist wooden galleries with blinds and brilliant multicolored ceramic work reminiscent of Antoni Gaudí's Casa Batlló. The interior of the building is equally dramatic with mosaic paving and superb furniture featuring uncommonly shaped benches. The main façade is a sharp contrast to the colorful display of the rear, with austere modern lines and built in monochromatic stone.

The Casa Comalat stands much the same as it did in the early twentieth century, although in this color photograph the polychromatic mosaic design of the building can be fully appreciated. The building was part of a massive restoration project by the Institute of Urban Landscaping via the city hall of Barcelona. The campaign took place between 1986 and 2004 and was called "¡Barcelona, possa't guapa!" (Barcelona, make yourself pretty!). The purpose was to provide funds for the technical assessment, renovation, and official protection of edifices considered part of the city's architectural heritage. The Institute provided funds for the recent renovation of Casa Comalat's roof.

Lluís Domènech i Montaner was commissioned to design this building on Aragó Street by his cousin Ramón de Montaner and his partner Francesc Simo. The challenge was to build an aesthetically pleasing industrial building in the middle of a residential area (very close to fashionable Passeig de Gràcia). It was constructed between 1881 and 1886 and at the time was considered one of the first official Modernist-style buildings, although the façade of the building is not representative of the Modernist movement as it is understood today. Built with brick in a neo-Arab style, which was popular at the time, the building incorporates elements of hand-wrought iron and glass and is crowned with busts and stone adornments.

The building was acquired by the city hall of Barcelona in 1987 and donated to Fundació Antoni Tapies, a museum dedicated to the famous Catalan artist Antoni Tapies, which opened to the public in 1990. It was completely renovated to house the museum. Antoni Tapies, whose artistic work has historically been innovative and controversial, felt that the building was unjustly overshadowed by its two neighboring structures. To overcome this difference in height he created the chaotic wire sculpture *Núvol i Cadira* (*Cloud and Chair*) for the roof. Antoni Tapies, born in 1923, continues to produce artwork and has published several collections of essays on the subjects of art and aesthetics.

Casa Milà, or as it is popularly known, la Pedrera ("the stone quarry") was designed in 1905 and under construction until 1911. This majestic building made of blocks of local garraf stone stands on the upper part of Barcelona's stately main street, Passeig de Gràcia. It was the last private house designed by Antoni Gaudí. Gaudí designed the apartment block with not a single straight line on the interior or exterior of the building. The result is a mountainous, graceful structure that, while technically Modernist, contains hints of the Expressionist period that would soon follow. In this early photo, construction is not quite complete; the emblematic abstract iron railings have yet to be fitted onto the balconies.

Upon its completion in 1911 the Casa Milà was reported for exceeding the total volume of space permitted by zoning laws of the time. While there was a brief debate over whether it would be necessary to remove part of the penthouse to comply with these rules, the owners were soon granted an exception to the law in view of the remarkable nature of the building. Today the Casa Milà stands completed and in excellent condition. There are still several privately owned apartments in the building, as well as a typical apartment converted into a museum showcasing the curved design of the blocks. The roof, with its chimneys and ventilators, has become the building's crowning glory. There is a surreal avant-garde stone garden made from the unusual forms. The roof is open to the public and in summertime hosts jazz concerts.

The Casa Fuster, pictured here in 1932, originated as a lavish gift from Mariano Fuster i Fuster to his wife Consuelo Fabra i Puig, daughter of the Marqués de Alella. The building was designed by architect Lluís Domènech i Montaner, also famous for his Palau de la Música. He designed the house in his trademark Modernist style with intricate ornamentation and attention to detail. Building began in 1908 and was completed in 1911 when the Fuster i Fabra family moved into the main floor. At the time, the house was the most expensive in the city because of its prime location on the Passeig de Gràcia and the high-quality white marble used to create the façade. Also pictured here is a fountain dedicated to Minerva.

The family was unable to keep up with the high cost of maintaining the house and was forced to move out in the 1920s. From then until 1962 it was known as Café Vienés and housed a string of small businesses, including a barber shop and a popular dance hall called El Danubio Azul. In 1962 an electric company bought Casa Fuster with the intention of tearing it down to build a skyscraper. In response to fierce public opposition the company changed its plans and instead opted to restore the building to its original glory. The most recent restoration was in 1995, and in the year 2000 Casa Fuster was bought by a hotel chain and converted into a deluxe five-star hotel. The Minerva fountain was dismantled in 1933.

This palace in the Eixample was commissioned by the Baron of Quadras and designed by the famed Modernist architect Joesp Puig i Cadafalch in 1904. Puig i Cadafalch was the architect for the refurbishment of the baron's mansion in Maçanet, and upon its completion the baron requested his services for the project of a sumptuous residence in the capital city. Construction was completed in 1906. Puig i Cadafalch had to work within the confines of what was once a narrow apartment block typical of the Eixample. The exquisite and elegant results of his design are evident in both the interior and exterior of the building, which are rich with detailed Gothic ornaments and floral motifs.

The palace is now a fitting home to Casa Asia, an institution founded in 2001 with the goal of promoting relations between Spain and Asia in institutional, cultural, academic, and economic areas. Casa Asia was officially installed in the palace on June 16, 2003, and its opening ceremony was presided over by Prince Philip. The interior of the palace lends itself beautifully to the subject, as the detail-rich preserved walls and flooring give the building an Oriental feel. It houses an extensive resource center with information on all of Asia and a café that serves Asian food and drinks.

This Modernist building, known to locals as Casa de les Punxes, was built between 1903 and 1905 by Josep Puig i Cadafalch on the newly constructed Avinguda Diagonal. This photograph was taken soon after its completion. The Casa Terrades was named for the original owners, the Terrades sisters. Although it appears to be one unified structure, it is actually composed of three separate living spaces. The building boasts four rounded towers ending in *punxes* (sharp points). The brick façade displays ceramic panels with patriotic motifs, the most famous of which features Saint George, patron saint of Catalonia, and reads "Sant Patró de Catalunya, torneu-nos la llibertat" (Patron saint of Catalonia, return liberty to us). The panel was extremely provocative at a time when the Catalonian identity was mercilessly repressed by the government, but somehow the panel escaped removal and destruction.

The building underwent extensive renovations and restoration at the end of the 1980s, but its outward appearance remains almost unchanged. Today, what was once the spacious living quarters of the three sisters now houses a number of boutiques, a furniture store, and a kiosk. The most striking development in the picture is that of the street, Avinguda Diagonal, which fulfilled its intended purpose as part of the expansion of the city and is now one of the most widely used and commercialized streets in Barcelona.

La Sagrada Familia, the most famous building in Barcelona and the masterpiece of Modernist architect Antoni Gaudí, has a long and turbulent history. In 1881 an association of devout Catholics bought a plot of land in a quiet rural area to build a temple. This 1906 photograph shows an image of the church before its towers and façades were built, when the area was still a suitable place for goats. Under the supervision of the original architect, Francesc del Villar, plans for a church containing three naves commenced in 1882. But in 1883 del Villar fell out with the association and supervision was transferred to Antoni Gaudí, who created an entirely new design based on a basilical plan: five naves and a dome 550 feet high dedicated to Jesus Christ. Gaudí worked on the project for more than forty years until his death in 1926.

Work on the Sagrada Familia progresses at good pace now. Construction ceased at the start of the Spanish civil war (1936–39) and was further compromised when portions of the building, along with Gaudí's models and workshop, were destroyed by anarchists. Building recommenced after the war and continues today, following plans based on Gaudí's original designs as well as reconstructions of lost plans and modern adaptations by other architects. Because the original plans are unclear and open to interpretation, each new piece of the temple that is completed sparks debate over whether the construction has remained true to Gaudí's intentions. Estimates for the completion of the basilica vary widely.

This photograph from 1930 shows Plaça Tetuan at the intersection of the main streets Gran Via and Passeig de Sant Joan at a time when tramways were an important means of transportation. Passeig de Sant Joan, a project that was part of the ambitious Eixample expansion of Barcelona, was meant to be the second-most-important boulevard after Passeig de Gràcia, but it never quite lived up to these expectations.

The plaza is a major rotary, where the tramways have disappeared and were replaced by a modern metro system and large volumes of automobile traffic. The center of the plaza is popular with both children and elderly residents, boasting a playground and a popular petanca court. In the middle of the square, barely visible among the trees, is Josep Llimona's sculpture dedicated to Doctor Robert, a mayor of Barcelona in the late nineteenth century. The monument, a symbol for Catalan patriots, was originally located on Plaça Universitat, then dismantled after the civil war was won by the fascists. It was restored here in 1988, more than a decade after Spain had reestablished a democratic government.

The Plaça Monumental is a bullring designed by architects Ignasi Mas i Morell and Domènec Sugranyes. It was inaugurated in 1914 with the appearances of renowned bullfighters of the time. The ring was christened "El Sport" upon its opening, but was renamed "Monumental" in 1916. At the time of its opening the ring was considered one of the most prestigious in Spain, along with Las Ventas in Madrid and La Maestranza in Seville.

The ring occupies an entire city block on the edge of the Eixample neighborhood between streets Marina and Gran Via. The bullring was built in neo-Arab and Byzantine style using exposed brick and ceramic tiles. Constructed at the height of the Modernist era, these influences are visible in the egg-shaped cupolas that crown the top of the building.

The controversial sport of bullfighting is no longer as popular as it once was in Catalonia, or as it continues to be in other parts of Spain. The Monumental is the last arena that holds bullfighting events in the city of Barcelona. In addition to bullfights held every weekend during summer months, the plaza hosts cultural and musical events. The plaza featured the first and only appearance of the Beatles in Barcelona on July 3, 1965, and other musical greats who have performed here include the Rolling Stones, Bob Marley, Queen, and Bruce Springsteen. The ring is also home to the Museo Taurino de Barcelona, a museum honoring the tradition and spectacle of bullfighting in Spain, with exhibitions of costumes belonging to famous bullfighters in history, celebrated trophy bull heads, and historical documents related to the sport.

The main entrance to the enormous complex known as Hospital de Sant Pau lies on the edge of the Eixample neighborhood at the intersection of Sant Antoni Maria Claret Street and Cartagena Street in what was an area just outside of Barcelona city. The complex measures nine city blocks. The project began with a posthumous donation of four million pesetas ($31,000) by banker Pau Gil i Serra, in 1892, for a public hospital for the citizens of Barcelona, to be named after Saint Paul. It was begun by famed Modernist architect Lluís Domènech i Montaner in 1901, and although two optimistic mosaics at the entrance declare that construction began in 1905 and was finished in 1910—shortly before this 1912 photograph—construction wasn't completed until 1930. The original plan for the hospital involved the creation of forty-eight separate pavilions for different types of illnesses and treatments; however, the plans were simplified and only twenty-seven pavilions were eventually erected.

The present-day hospital remains one of the city's principal public-health facilities. In the photo one can see a more polished-looking entrance flanked by stately palm trees. On the staircase just beyond the wrought-iron gates there is a statue of the hospital's benefactor, Pau Gil i Serra, added in 1930. The hospital's pavilions underwent renovations and restoration several years ago, and there was a near-tragedy in 2004 when the heavy cupola that adorned the waiting room ceiling in the gynecology pavilion crashed to the ground and through the middle of the floor to the basement. Miraculously, due to the circular shape of the waiting room, all of the chairs were placed in a circle around the wall, so waiting patients and visitors escaped with only minor injuries. Subsequent inspections of the other facilities of the Hospital de Sant Pau found that three additional pavilions were structurally unsound and have been slated for renovation.

The signature fountain on Plaça d'Espanya was created by Josep Maria Jujol as an homage to Spain and a tribute to water for the International Exposition of 1929. The fountain's three main sculptures represent some of Spain's most important rivers: the Tajo, the Ebro, and the Guadalquivir, and another group of sculptures symbolizes Abundance, Health, and Navigation. Unfortunately, the water didn't flow on May 19, 1929, the day of the inauguration of the Expo, and the statues hadn't been placed, despite the momentous efforts to have the fountain finished on time. What the fountain did provide was an elevated area for people to climb and see the inaugural ceremony that took place across the square. Also visible in this picture, taken in 1930, is the bullring Arenas de Barcelona, just behind the fountain.

After the 1929 exposition, the terrible winds of the Spanish civil war blew against the fountain's columns, ironically dedicated to Heroism, Religion, and Art. During the frequent bombings of the period, people used the interior of the monument as a makeshift shelter. In the following years, some of the lanterns that adorned the exterior broke and some simply disappeared, leaving this landmark in a state of disrepair. The 1992 Olympic Games were the perfect excuse to refurbish the fountain on Plaça d'Espanya, one of the first sites visitors encounter as they arrive in Barcelona from the airport. Bullfighting has declined in popularity in Barcelona in recent decades and the former bullring Las Arenas is now in the process of being renovated, modernized, and reinvented as upscale retail and office space. The building to the right of the bullring is a hotel.

Up from Plaça d'Espanya, toward the hill of Montjuic, we find Avinguda Maria Cristina. The street furniture of the avenue was updated in time for the 1929 International Exposition and a fountain was built at the corner with Avinguda Marques de Comillas. The fountain's ever-changing water jets produced up to thirty different combinations in different colors, and the

"Magical Fountain" became one of the main attractions during the Expo. The imposing Palau Nacional's main façade, at the end of the avenue, had spotlights installed behind it, and the illuminated obelisks on both sides of the avenue made it a spectacular location both day and night in the 1930s.

The Palau Nacional still presides over Avinguda Maria Cristina and currently houses the MNAC, or Museum of National Art of Catalonia. This avenue is the central artery of Barcelona's Trade Fair and remains very busy during the day whenever there is a convention in town. The frenetic business activity ceases when the sun sets and the fountain fills the urban nights with an unforgettable show of color and—from 1976 onward—music. The addition of sound technology is only one in a series of renovations the Magical Fountain has undergone during the twentieth century. The obelisks in the previous picture deteriorated during the civil war and eventually disappeared. In 1980 they were replaced by water jets.

These four imposing columns at the base of Montjuic mountain represent the four red stripes of the Catalan flag. One legend has it that the flag's design originated from a particularly bloody battle in the fourteenth century, after which Ramón Berenguer, Count of Barcelona, wiped his blood-stained fingers on his golden shield, thus inspiring the design for the yellow- and red-striped flag. The work was created in 1919 by Josep Puig i Cadafalch, when he was the president of the Mancomunitat de Catalunya. Each column was more than sixty-five feet high and six feet wide, and crowned by Ionic capitals. In the background the then-popular bullring Las Arenas is visible.

In 1928 the dictator Primo de Rivera, wishing to subdue independent sentiments in the region of Catalonia, had the columns demolished so they would not be seen by visitors to the upcoming International Exposition. The two Venetian-style brick towers were created as the entrance to the Expo; behind them is the Hotel Plaza. The avenue leading down to Plaça d'Espanya is Avinguda Maria Cristina. On both sides of this avenue is the "Fira de Barcelona," or trade show area.

This 1929 picture shows the famous Barcelona Pavilion, which was designed by Ludwig Mies van der Rohe to serve as the German national pavilion during the 1929 Barcelona International Exposition. The building was originally conceived as the site of the reception given by the German authorities and presided over by King Alfonso XIII of Spain, the grandfather of Spain's current monarch. The main materials used in its construction were glass and marble. The pavilion was dismantled in 1930, once the exposition ended, but as time went by it became a symbol of twentieth-century architecture for conveying the ideal of modernity.

This identical but newly rebuilt Mies van der Rohe Pavilion stands again on its original site on the slopes of the hill of Montjuic, attracting architects and architectural students every year. The idea of reconstructing the building had gained momentum over the years and in 1980 was brought to fruition by Oriol Bohigas, the head of the city's Urban Planning Department. Architects

Ignasi de Solà-Morales, Cristian Cirici, and Fernando Ramos were responsible for developing the project, which used the same materials as the original building by Mies van der Rohe. Construction began in 1983 and the site was opened to visitors in 1986.

Montjuic had not yet hosted the 1929 International Exposition when Casimir Casaramona, a successful local businessman, commissioned Modernist architect Josep Puig i Cadafalch to build his new textile factory at the foot of the mountain. The factory was finished in 1911 and the city hall awarded it a prize as one of the city's best constructions the very next year. Casaramona's previous factory had been destroyed by a fire, so the new building boasted the most modern fire prevention technology available at the time. Each tower contained huge water tanks for use in case of a fire.

The life of this beautiful state-of-the-art facility was short. Casaramona died the same year the plant opened and the factory closed in 1920, after only seven years in existence. The building served various purposes in the following decades, including that of police headquarters, and then in 1963 it was acquired by a major Catalan bank. The financial institution undertook the renovation of the building and turned it into today's Caixa Forum, a museum of contemporary art and cultural center. The renovation maintained the original appearance of the building, one of the most stunning examples of Modernist industrial architecture. The Casaramona Factory was declared a Historic Artistic Monument in 1976.

This stadium, located on the mountain Montjuic, was built for the International Exposition in Barcelona in 1929. Pictured here is the 1952 International Eucharist Congress. The congress brought together thousands of devout Catholics in Barcelona at a low point in history for the Catalan people. During the period following the civil war, Barcelona was still a city greatly affected by the tragedies of the past decades and struggling to recover. The congress tried to address some of the city's social problems, particularly the housing shortage. Pictured here is the famous ceremony during which 820 priests were ordained, the largest ordination of this kind in history.

The Expo stadium is now named Estadi Olímpic Lluís Companys, for Catalan politician Lluís Companys i Jover (1882–1940), who is buried in the nearby cemetery Cementiri del Sud-Oest. It was recently extensively remodeled to accommodate the 1992 Summer Olympic Games. In 1998 the Football Stadium Committee awarded the stadium a five-star rating, signifying that it was suitable for the highest level of continental soccer matches. It is now the official stadium of the Espanyol soccer team and is used for a variety of cultural events. It also served as the home of the Barcelona Dragons American Football team until 2003. The stadium has a capacity of 54,000 people for sports events and 68,000 for concerts.

This bleak view of Barcelona in 1903 is from Miramar (*mira* means "look," and *mar*, "sea"), a viewing point on the hill of Montjuic. Barcelona was the industrial capital of Catalonia, and the districts of Poble Sec and the Raval at the foot of the hill housed many big factories and mills, largely from the textile industry. The factories' tall brick chimneys blew great continuous plumes of black smoke over the city, covering all buildings in the vicinity with soot and creating massive pollution. The tall, slender tower to the left of the most prominent chimney is the Christopher Columbus monument.

Gradually, at the start of the twentieth century, factories began moving to the outskirts of the city and to neighboring suburbs, first due to a of lack of space in Barcelona, then in later years to comply with the local zoning laws that restricted noise and pollution. Apartment buildings replaced the old mills, and Barcelona is now largely a service-oriented city with tourism and telecommunications as the driving forces of the economy. This vastly improved panorama of the city allows the visitor a clear view at the pleasant blue sea for which the outlook was named. Columbus still stands in the center of the picture, now sharing the skyline with the 1992 towers of the Olympic compound in the distance.

Plaça Rius i Taulet, also known popularly as La Plaça del Rellotge, or the Clock Square, was named for a nineteenth-century liberal mayor of Barcelona, Francesc de Paula Rius i Taulet, who was largely responsible for Barcelona hosting the 1888 Exposition. The bell tower was constructed 140 years ago by architect Antoni Rovira i Trias to stand in front of what was then the town hall of Gràcia. The clock was constructed with four faces in order to be visible from all points in the plaza. Residents consider the bell tower to be a symbol of freedom and democracy because it played a key role in alerting the townspeople to public revolts in 1870, 1873, and 1874. The bell itself was the center of controversy when it was "borrowed" by the city of Barcelona in 1929 for another tower built for the World Expo until angry Gràcia residents demanded its restitution.

The square is the center of the neighborhood of Gràcia, a traditionally progressive district of Barcelona that was once a separate town and still exhibits some of its individualistic spirit in the colorful and quirky buildings, outdoor bars, and annual festivals for which it is famous. The bell tower remains intact both inside and out. Once a month the tower is open to the public so that visitors may climb up and see the bell at close quarters, but this excursion is not for the faint of heart: the interior of the tower still encases the original narrow spiral staircase that, due to spatial constraints, has neither landings for resting nor railings for balance.

This image shows the Vallcarca bridge in 1926 soon after it was built. Vallcarca, close to Gaudí's Park Güell, is a valley (*Vall* means "valley" in Catalan) on the outskirts of Barcelona just beyond the district of Gràcia. It lies between two hills: Turo del Coll and Turo del Putxet. At the time of the photograph it was well outside the city and known as a summer town, where many residents of Barcelona built pleasant cottages to have a place outside of the bustle of the city.

Vallcarca—which used to have its own specific identity, along with the neighboring villas of Gràcia and Horta—has gradually been absorbed into the city of Barcelona and fallen victim to the city's booming real estate market. Dwellings once considered summer homes now share extremely close quarters with high-rise apartment buildings or have been demolished to make room for new and more lucrative construction projects. The two hills that border the area and were once dotted with the occasional summer residence in the woods are now almost as densely populated as the city center that Vallcarca's original residents sought to escape.

This remarkable Modernist building perches on top of Balmes, at the bottom of Avinguda Tibidabo. Balmes is in Sarria, a neighborhood known as the *part alta* or "high part" of the city, which reflects both the altitude due to close proximity to Mount Tibidabo and the social class of the neighborhood's residents, both in the past and the present. La Rotonda was built by Adolf Ruiz i Casamitjana in 1906 as the once luxurious Hotel Metropolitan.

La Rotonda lies on the famous Tibidabo Avenue. Next to the building is the stop for the Tramvia Blau (Blue Tramway), one of the earliest public transportation systems in Barcelona. The Tramvia was inaugurated in 1901 as part of an ambitious project to create a theme park at the top of Tibidabo that would require easy public access to the peak of the mountain.

In form, if not function, La Rotonda remains largely unchanged. The building has been well maintained and is now used as a private health clinic. The Tramvia Blau is still up and running and serves its original purpose as the easiest and most practical means of transportation for reaching the top of

Tibidabo. Not only is the tramway practical, but it is picturesque as well: its slow and steady ascent allows passengers a pleasant view of the grand mansions—many now converted from private residences into offices or restaurants—that line the Avinguda Tibidabo.

Near the top of Mount Tibidabo lies Plaça Dr. Andreu, named for Salvador Andreu i Grau, an industrial pharmacist whose financial success led him into urban development ventures. He initiated the ambitious project of building a funicular railway that would transport passengers from the end of the tramway to the peak of Tibidabo. The funicular's first journey took place on July 3, 1901, with Dr. Andreu as the sole passenger. The path of the funicular is 3,750 feet long, and the original wooden carriages that held eighty passengers were divided into first class and economy class.

Funicular services were briefly interrupted in January 1958 so that the wooden carriages could be replaced by metal ones, and their capacity increased to 227 passengers. The funicular proved so popular that two years later, in 1960, a new machine was built that could complete the journey in only six minutes and thereby transport up to 1,500 passengers per hour. Both the original.and modern versions of the funicular are preserved and still take visitors to the top of Tibidabo, where there is a theme park. The plaza itself is also a popular destination for its privileged views of the city. Traditional Catalan restaurant La Venta, at right in the photograph, offers spectacular vistas of the Barcelona sky and sea.

The palace behind the gates to the right in this early 1930s photograph is the Palau Reial, built for King Alfonso XIII in 1929. Located on the upper section of Barcelona's wide and stately Avinguda Diagonal, the palace was once part the estate that belonged to the prominent Güell family (commissioners of Gaudí's Park Güell) where they lived in their residence Can Cuyàs. The land for the palace was ceded to the royal family in the 1920s for the purpose of constructing a residence for their visits to Barcelona. Work began in 1921, and the majority of the upper classes made economic contributions toward the construction, as well as numerous donations of important artwork from their private collections for the interior of the royal palace. King Alfonso XIII was driven into exile in 1931 when Spain declared itself a republic.

The outside gate of the Palau Reial is little changed, although the inside is no longer a royal residence but a museum of decorative arts, showcasing the majority of the royal collection. This area of Avinguda Diagonal, once a country setting far outside the bustling capital, has been extensively developed. The surrounding neighborhood, now known as the "Zona Universitaria," is the result of the expansion of the University of Barcelona. The university acquired land in the Pedralbes district next to the palace in 1952. The area now called the Pedralbes Campus houses students and the faculties of pharmacy, law, business, and economics.

This extensive and imaginative medieval-style castle was actually built in
1929. El Cuartell del Bruc, located in what was at the time the countryside,
was a project conceived to lodge the infantry brigade that was previously
concentrated in other barracks such as San Fernando and Buensuceso. At
the time of construction the project had a budget of 6.5 million pesetas
(about $50,000) and was built to house six hundred men.

The Cuartell del Bruc is one of the few grand buildings of Barcelona that continues in its original role. Today it is still used by the military, though no longer as the garrison for the infantry brigade. While the building has remained unaltered, the district around it has changed considerably in the last decades and has burgeoned into the exclusive neighborhood of Pedralbes, one of Barcelona's most prosperous suburbs.

The Camp de les Corts was home to the Barcelona Football club from 1922 to 1957. Inaugurated on May 20, 1922, the stadium had a capacity of 30,000 that was later doubled to 60,000. The 1920s is considered a golden age for F.C. Barcelona, who won the Catalan championship every year from 1923 to 1928 as well as three Spanish Championships. The picture shown here corresponds to that time period. The roster boasted renowned players such as Samitier, Alcántara, Zamora, Sagi, Piera, and Sancho, and the team's popularity steadily increased. Supporters of F.C. Barcelona were more than just soccer fans, however: the club was also considered a symbol of Catalan pride during a time when the Catalan identity and language began to be repressed by Spanish nationalists.

F.C. Barcelona's current home, built near the old Camp de les Corts is the Camp Nou stadium (literally named the New Field), which was opened on September 24, 1957. The new stadium had a capacity of 90,000 and was the perfect home for a team who had just won the latest Spanish Cup. During the rule of General Franco, the club's importance grew—because of its championship victories as well as for its social significance. Until the death of Franco in 1975, Catalans lived in a dictatorship that forbade popular manifestations of Catalan culture, including celebrations and the Catalan language. The sport became one of the only accepted public forums where people could show support for their region, and games between Barcelona and rival Real Madrid were fraught with political tension that continues to the present day. The stadium also houses a museum chronicling the history of the team.

This Gothic monastery, with the emblematic arches and columns, is located in the upper part of Barcelona and was founded by King James II and his wife Elisenda de Moncada in 1326. It was formally opened with a high mass on May 3, 1327, and was occupied by nuns of Saint Clare, a Franciscan order largely composed of the daughters of nobility. Thanks to Queen Elisenda, the monastery enjoyed protection from the city in case of attacks. This protection agreement was put into effect more than three hundred years later during the 1640 war, when the Mother Superior was forced to close the monastery and the sisters were hidden from the soldiers by the city council in the private residence of the Marqués de Aitona.

The outside of the monastery was originally fortified, but only two watchtowers have been conserved over the centuries. The monastery was declared a Historic Artistic Monument in 1991, and a small community of nuns from the Order of St. Clare still lives in a modern wing nearby. The building was used as a museum to display artworks from the Thyssen collection; it is now a part of the Museum of City History and offers a detailed look at the long history of the monastery, including the way of life for the nuns and the story of Queen Elisenda.

The Cathedral, a jewel of medieval architecture situated in the heart of Barcelona's Gothic Quarter and visited by millions of people every year, stands in a state of semi-abandonment and neglect in this photograph from 1887. Initial construction of Barcelona's cathedral began in 1298 and continued at a steady pace for more than two centuries. In the sixteenth century, priority was given to finishing the interior, particularly the choir, where the Chapter of the Golden Fleece met in 1519, presided over by the mighty emperor Charles V. This meeting is considered by many to be the precursor of today's United Nations. The façade and the dome were left unfinished for hundreds of years.

In 1882, a wealthy banker named Manuel Girona personally undertook the completion of the Cathedral's façade in time for the Universal Exposition of 1888. The result is the current façade, which consists of the portal, the dome, two flank towers, and various spires and other ornamental elements. Architect Josep Oriol Mestre created a neo-Gothic design inspired by the original plans drawn up in 1408 and never carried out. The dome is 230 feet high and the bell towers reach 173 feet. The cathedral's façade was finished in 1888 and the dome in 1909. On October 4, 1997, the Cathedral held the wedding of Princess Cristina of Spain, second eldest daughter of King Juan Carlos, to F.C. Barcelona handball player, Iñaki Urdangarín.

INDEX